SUPER BOWL
PITTSBURGH STEELERS
CHAMPIONS

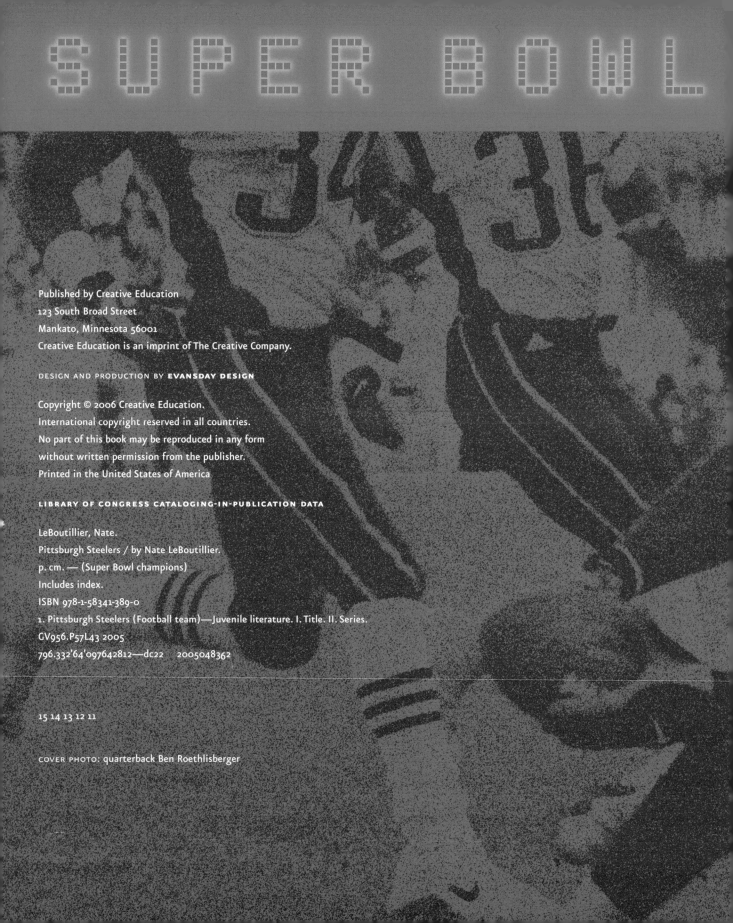

SUPER BOWL

Published by Creative Education
123 South Broad Street
Mankato, Minnesota 56001
Creative Education is an imprint of The Creative Company.

DESIGN AND PRODUCTION BY **EVANSDAY DESIGN**

LIBRARY OF CONGRESS CATALOGING-IN-PUBLICATION DATA

LeBoutillier, Nate.
Pittsburgh Steelers / by Nate LeBoutillier.
p. cm. — (Super Bowl champions)
Includes index.
ISBN 978-1-58341-389-0
1. Pittsburgh Steelers (Football team)—Juvenile literature. I. Title. II. Series.
GV956.P57L43 2005
796.332'64'097642812—dc22   2005048362

15 14 13 12 11

COVER PHOTO: quarterback Ben Roethlisberger

CHAMPIONS

PITTSBURGH STEELERS

THE STEELERS are a professional football team in the National Football League (NFL). They play in Pittsburgh, Pennsylvania. The weather can be cold in Pittsburgh. But the Steelers and their fans do not seem to mind.

THE STEELERS play in a stadium called Heinz Field. Their helmets are black with yellow, orange, and blue diamond shapes on the side. Their uniforms are black and gold. The Steelers play many games against teams called the Bengals, Browns, and Ravens.

THE STEELERS played their first season in 1933. At first, the Steelers were not very good. But when they hired a coach named Chuck Noll in 1969, they got a lot better.

ONE OF the Steelers' best players was Terry Bradshaw. He was a quarterback with a strong throwing arm. He helped make the Steelers a tough team. Today, Terry Bradshaw talks about football on TV.

THE STEELERS played a famous game against the Oakland Raiders in 1972. The game was almost over, and the Raiders were winning. But then Steelers running back Franco Harris saw a pass bounce off another player. He grabbed it and raced in for a touchdown to win the game. It was the Steelers' first win in the playoffs.

THE STEELERS' defense was so tough that fans called it "The Steel Curtain." Scoring touchdowns against the Steelers was hard work.

JOE GREENE was one of the Steelers' best players on defense. He was tall and used his big body to tackle quarterbacks and running backs. Fans called him "Mean Joe Greene."

The Steelers used their best plays against the Cowboys ^

THE **STEELERS** won the Super Bowl four times in the 1970s. No team had ever won four Super Bowls before. The Steelers beat teams called the Vikings, the Cowboys (twice), and the Rams.

TODAY, Ben Roethlisberger (*Roth-liss-ber-ger*) is the Steelers' quarterback. In his rookie season, the Steelers almost got to the Super Bowl. In 2005, the Steelers won the Super Bowl by beating a team called the Seahawks. In 2008, the Steelers beat a team called the Cardinals to win their sixth Super Bowl. They were world champions again!

GLOSSARY

National Football League (NFL)

a group of football teams that play against each other;
there are 32 teams in the NFL today

playoffs

games played after a season to see which team
is the best

professional

a person or team that gets paid to play or work

rookie

a player in his first season in the NFL

FUN FACTS

Team colors
Black and gold

Home stadium
Heinz Field (64,450 seats)

Conference/Division
American Football Conference (AFC), North Division

First season
1933

Super Bowl wins
1974 (beat Minnesota Vikings 16–6)
1975 (beat Dallas Cowboys 21–17)
1978 (beat Dallas Cowboys 35–31)
1979 (beat Los Angeles Rams 31–19)
2005 (beat Seattle Seahawks 21–10)
2008 (beat Arizona Cardinals 27–23)

Training camp location
Latrobe, Pennsylvania

Steelers Web site for kids
http://www.steelers.com/kidsclub/

NFL Web site for kids
http://www.playfootball.com

INDEX